The World of
SHARKS

GREAT WHITE SHARKS
HAMMERHEAD SHARKS
MAKO SHARKS
NURSE SHARKS
WHALE SHARKS
THRESHER SHARKS

Written by Sarah Palmer
Illustrated by Ernest Nicol and Libby Turner

DERRYDALE BOOKS
New York

Originally published in six separate volumes under the titles:
Great White Sharks, copyright © 1988 Rourke Enterprises, Inc.
Hammerhead Sharks, copyright © 1988 Rourke Enterprises, Inc.
Mako Sharks, copyright © 1988 Rourke Enterprises, Inc.
Nurse Sharks, copyright © 1988 Rourke Enterprises, Inc.
Whale Sharks, copyright © 1988 Rourke Enterprises, Inc.
Thresher Sharks, copyright © 1988 Rourke Enterprises, Inc.
All rights reserved.
This 1990 edition is published by Derrydale Books,
distributed by Outlet Book Company, Inc., a Random House Company,
225 Park Avenue South, New York, New York 10003, by arrangement
with Rourke Enterprises, Inc.

Printed and bound in the United States of America

Library of Congress Cataloging-in-Publication Data

Palmer, Sarah, 1955–
     World of sharks / by Sarah Palmer.
          p.   cm.
     Originally published separately under titles: Great white sharks ;
Hammerhead sharks ; Mako sharks ; Nurse sharks ; Whale sharks ;
Thresher sharks.
Vero Beach, FL : Rourke Enterprises, c1988. (Shark discovery
library).
     Summary: Describes the physical characteristics, habitat, and
behavior of five different kinds of sharks.
     ISBN 0-517-02747-X
     1. Sharks—Juvenile literature.   [1. Sharks.]   I. Title.
QL638.9.P34   1990
597'.31—dc20   90-3726
                                                                    CIP
                                                                    AC

8   7   6   5   4   3   2   1

TABLE OF CONTENTS

GREAT WHITE SHARKS

GREAT WHITE SHARKS

The most famous story about a great white shark is *Jaws*. The story tells how a savage great white shark killed and frightened people on the beaches of New England. Great white sharks are the most dangerous of all sharks. It is said that they are designed only for killing. Luckily, great white sharks are not as common as other, less harmful, sharks.

"Jaws" was a story about a savage great white shark

HOW THEY LOOK

Great white sharks have brownish gray backs with pale gray or white undersides. Their **pectoral fins** are tipped with black. An average female great white shark grows to about 15 feet long. Female sharks are usually bigger than the males. The largest great white shark known was nearly 30 feet long. It would have weighed about 4 tons.

Great white sharks can grow to be 30 feet long

WHERE THEY LIVE

Great white sharks live in warm seas. In the summer they can be found in the more northern areas of the Atlantic Ocean, like New England and New Jersey. In the winter these great white sharks **migrate** south along the eastern seaboard to the Gulf of Mexico and the South Atlantic Ocean. Great whites can be found in warm, shallow bays in many countries.

Great white sharks like shallow waters

WHAT THEY EAT

All sharks are **carnivorous**, or flesh-eating. Great white sharks will eat almost any kind of flesh, whether alive or dead. They eat large fish, seals, sea lions, turtles, and even dead whales. Two whole sea lions were found inside the body of one 16-foot shark. Many great whites are found off the coast of California, where there are seal colonies on which they can **prey** for food.

A great white shark attacks a sea lion

Great white sharks are very dangerous

Some people fish for great white sharks

THEIR JAWS AND TEETH

Great white sharks have very strong jaws and huge teeth. The teeth in the sharks' upper jaws are triangular and can grow up to 3 inches long. The teeth are narrower in the lower jaws. Each tooth has a **serrated** edge like a saw, which makes them doubly sharp.

*Great white sharks' teeth are
very sharp*

SHARK ATTACK!

It is thought that great white sharks are responsible for about 4 in 10 shark attacks on humans. They attack more often than any other shark. One-third of the great white sharks' victims die from their injuries. Those who escape are often left with ugly scars from the sharks' teeth. Sometimes they may even lose an arm or a leg. It is easy to understand why people are so afraid of these sharks.

Great white sharks attack swiftly

HOW THEY ATTACK

Almost no one who has been attacked by a great white shark saw the fish coming. The first thing they knew was that a part of their body had been snatched by the shark. Some sharks circle their **prey** before an attack, but the great white shark moves in quickly and without warning. With the first strike, it will disable its prey. With the next, it seeks to kill and eat its **victim**.

*Great white sharks attack people
more often than any other shark*

AVOIDING SHARK ATTACKS

The risk of shark attack is very low. Nevertheless, you can reduce even further your chances of being attacked by how you act. You should never swim at beaches where sharks are common. Do not swim alone, especially at dusk or after dark, when the sharks are feeding. Do not wear bright jewelry or watches in the water. Never swim with an open wound, the blood will attract sharks.

Never wear bright jewelry when swimming

FACT FILE

Common Name: Great White Shark
Scientific Name: Carcharodon carcharias
Color: Brownish gray
Average Size: 11 feet, 4 inches
Where They Live: Warm waters, mostly offshore but also found in surf and shallow bays
Danger Level: Most dangerous shark

HAMMERHEAD SHARKS

HAMMERHEAD SHARKS

Five **species** of hammerhead sharks are found in the oceans around the United States. The three most common kinds are the Great Hammerhead, the Scalloped Hammerhead, and the Smalleye Hammerhead. All hammerhead sharks are very strange looking. Their heads are flattened and shaped like hammers. This is how they got their name.

A Great Hammerhead shark

HOW THEY LOOK

Hammerhead sharks range in size from an average of 11 feet, for the female Great Hammerhead, to 4 feet, for the Smalleye Hammerhead. The Great Hammerhead and the Scalloped Hammerhead are greenish brown, and the Smalleye Hammerhead is gray. They all have white undersides. The largest known hammerhead was a Great Hammerhead measuring over 18 feet, 7 inches.

From top to bottom: Smalleye, Great and Scalloped Hammerhead sharks

WHERE THEY LIVE

The Scalloped Hammerhead is the most common of the five species and is found in warm waters all over the world. The Great Hammerhead lives mostly in shallow **reefs**, although it is sometimes seen in quite deep waters. The little Smalleye Hammerhead stays in inshore waters, close to land. It has been known to live in fresh water·rivers.

*Great Hammerheads live mostly
in shallow lagoons*

WHAT THEY EAT

All hammerhead sharks eat bony fish, squid, crabs, and sometimes smaller sharks. The Great Hammerheads' favorite food is the stingray. Great Hammerheads are often found with the barbs from stingrays' tails in and around their mouths. One had as many as fifty stuck in his mouth. The Smalleye Hammerhead is known to eat baby Scalloped Hammerheads.

Smalleye Hammerheads sometimes eat baby Scalloped Hammerheads

*Hammerhead sharks are
considered dangerous*

Great Hammerhead sharks are a
greenish color

THEIR EYES

Hammerhead sharks' eyes are located on each end of their heads. Their eyelids slide up from the lower edge of their eyes to cover the sensitive eyeball. Hammerhead sharks' eyes usually close as they bite their **prey**, to protect them. Scientists used to think that sharks had poor eyesight. They now know that sharks can see quite well, even in dim light.

This picture shows the position of a hammerhead's eyes and nostrils

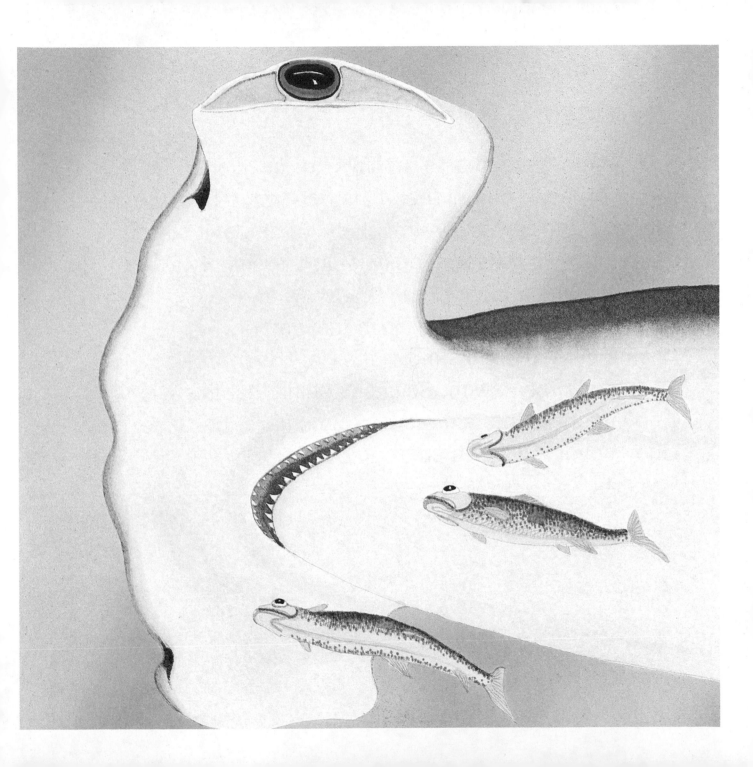

THEIR SENSES

Hammerhead sharks' nostrils are positioned far apart on each end of their hammer-shaped heads, close to their eyes. As the shark breathes, it takes water into its **gills** and nostrils. In the same way that humans find smells in the air when they breathe, sharks find smells in the water. Hammerhead sharks move their heads from side to side as they swim. Scientists think that this movement helps them to pick up smells, because they cover a wider area.

Hammerheads swing their heads from side to side as they swim

SHARK ATTACK!

Most hammerhead sharks are considered dangerous. When people are in trouble and are easy prey, they are often the first sharks to arrive. Hammerhead sharks arrive at the scene of a tragedy in large groups, or **schools**. Great Hammerheads are thought to be man-eaters. Scalloped Hammerheads have been blamed for some attacks on humans, but scientists have found them harmless in captivity.

43

A school of hammerhead sharks arrive at a shipwreck

AVOIDING SHARK ATTACK

At many beaches in the United States nets are set up to catch sharks who come too close to shore. The nets are placed in quite deep water parallel to the shoreline. If a shark swims into the net, he gets tangled up in it and dies. This is a good way of protecting swimmers, but it is not always so good for other sea life. Sometimes harmless dolphins and seals get caught up in the netting and die.

Hammerhead sharks can get caught in shark nets

FACT FILE

Common Name: Great Hammerhead Shark
Scientific Name: Sphyrna mokarran
Color: Greenish brown
Average Size: Male   – 9 feet, 4 inches
                   Female – 12 feet
Where They Live: Shallow waters around reefs
Danger Level: Dangerous shark

MAKO SHARKS

MAKO SHARKS

Mako sharks belong to the family of mackerel sharks. They are related to the feared great white shark. There are two kinds of mako sharks, the longfin mako and the shortfin mako. Mako sharks are the fastest moving sharks in the world, and one of the fastest fish. They can swim at over 22 miles per hour in short bursts.

Mako sharks can swim very fast

HOW THEY LOOK

Shortfin mako sharks have metallic blue backs with pure white undersides. Longfin makos are much darker, and have a blue-black skin. The largest known longfin mako was 12 feet, 8 inches long. The average size for a female of both **species** is 10 feet. Mako sharks have large **dorsal fins**. Their tail fins are designed for fast swimming: the upper and lower **lobes** are almost the same size.

A longfin and a shortfin mako

WHERE THEY LIVE

Mako sharks live in warm seas. Scientists have found that makos **migrate** to warmer waters in the winter, when the seas where they live cool off. They studied one shortfin mako that swam from the seas near Virginia all the way to the West Indies. That's a distance of 1,690 miles! Longfin makos usually live in deeper waters than shortfin makos.

Shortfin makos live in coral reefs

WHAT THEY EAT

Mako sharks will eat almost any kind of fish. They have been known to eat mackerel, tuna, herring and squid, as well as bigger fish like swordfish and marlins. Makos have dagger-like teeth, which are long and pointed with smooth edges. They use these sharp teeth to spear their **prey**.

Mako sharks sometimes eat swordfish

Shortfin makos can swim long distances

Mako sharks have large dorsal
fins

SHARK ATTACK!

Shortfin mako sharks are thought to be dangerous. They have been known to attack boats. Boats with white hulls seem to attract attacks by shortfin makos. Makos have been known to attack humans. Scientists warn that they could be deadly. When they are angry, these sharks attack with great strength.

A shortfin mako attacks a white-hulled boat

PREVENTING SHARK ATTACK

Scientists are still looking for the best way to keep sharks away from beaches. Some sharks still get through the nets and fences that are built to keep them away from swimmers. One idea is to use very loud noises to frighten away the sharks. Another system, which has been tested in South Africa, uses cables to produce electrical currents that the sharks will not cross.

A mako breaks through a shark net

IF A SHARK ATTACKS

A shark attack **victim** will suffer from loss of blood and from shock. The bleeding should be stopped as soon as possible. To bring the injured person out of shock, a greater flow of blood must reach his or her head. The person should be laid on the beach, positioned so the head is lower than the feet. He or she should be wrapped in a blanket until medical aid can arrive. Never try to move an injured person.

A shark victim is carried from the water

BABY MAKO SHARKS

There are three ways in which sharks produce their young. Some sharks lay eggs on the **seabed**, and from these eggs baby sharks hatch. Others produce eggs that they carry inside them until the babies are ready to hatch. Some sharks, like the mako, give birth to live young. Mako sharks normally have four babies each year.

Mako sharks bear live young

FACT FILE

Common Name: Shortfin Mako Shark
Scientific Name: Isurus oxyrinchus
Color: Metallic blue
Average Size: Male   – 7 feet, 10 inches
                   Female – 11 feet
Where They Live: Warm waters, mostly
                   offshore
Danger Level: Dangerous shark

NURSE SHARKS

NURSE SHARKS

Nurse sharks are slow and clumsy creatures. They do not move around as much as some sharks and are often found just lying on the **seabed**. Sometimes as many as thirty nurse sharks may be seen sleeping on top of each other. Nurse sharks are **nocturnal**. This means that they sleep during the day and are active only at night.

69

Nurse sharks can be found piled on top of one another

HOW THEY LOOK

Nurse sharks are yellowish gray on their backs. Young nurse sharks may have darker spots on their backs. Their undersides are lighter in color. Nurse sharks do not look as sleek as some of the other sharks. Their bodies are more rounded. The average size for a nurse shark is about 7 feet, 6 inches. Females are only a little bigger than the males.

Nurse sharks bodies are more rounded than other sharks

WHERE THEY LIVE

Nurse sharks can be found off the east and southwest coasts of the United States and near the west coast of Africa. They live on the ocean floor, usually quite close to the shore. Nurse sharks are sometimes found in deep water where the ocean is very cold. Nurse sharks do not seem to **migrate**, but as the water cools they become even less active.

Nurse sharks usually live deep in the water

WHAT THEY EAT

Nurse sharks eat squid, crabs, shrimp, fish, lobster, and even spiny sea urchins. They have hinged jaws and huge mouths. Nurse sharks suck prey into their enormous mouths and swallow everything whole. The tawny nurse shark, which is sometimes called the giant sleepy shark, can spit as well as suck. It may spit at you if you frighten it.

A nurse shark attacking a crustacean

Nurse sharks do not often attack
unless provoked

Nurse sharks like to stay near
the seabed

THEIR JAWS AND TEETH

The nurse sharks' hinged jaws and sharp teeth make them dangerous both to humans and to other fish. Once their jaws are tightly shut, it is difficult to get them to open their mouths again. Nurse sharks' teeth are long and pointed. They look as sharp as needles. Nurse sharks look more fierce than they really are.

Nurse shark's teeth are very sharp

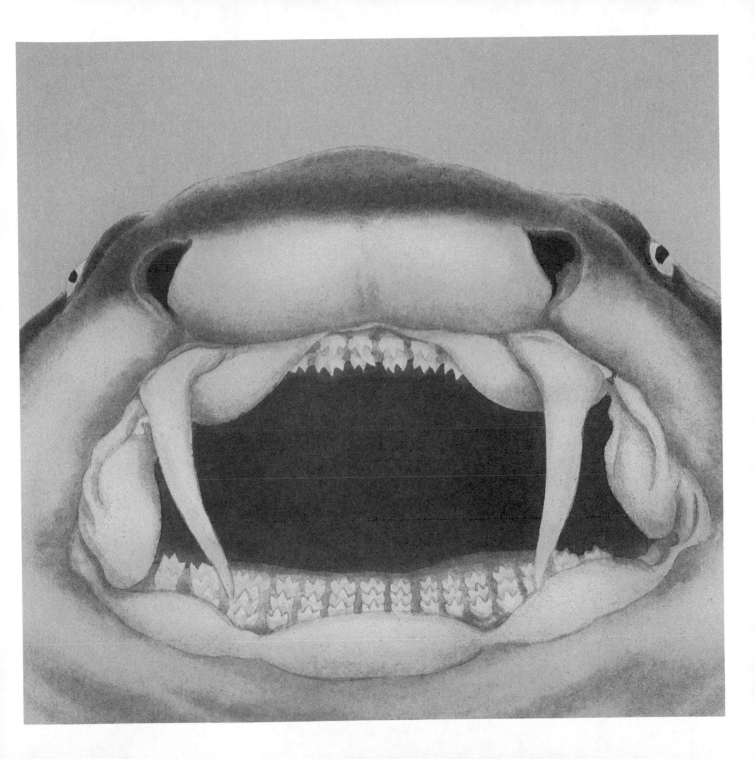

BABY NURSE SHARKS

Female nurse sharks are unusual, because they can either lay eggs or bear live young. Nurse sharks' eggs are 4 inches long when the young hatch from them. The mother shark does not look after her babies after they are born. She swims away and leaves them to find food for themselves.

Baby nurse sharks hatch from eggs

SHARK ATTACK!

Nurse sharks do not normally attack people, but if you make them angry or afraid, they will bite you. They snap quickly when they attack and do not let go easily. Because nurse sharks sleep in shallow water during the day, it is quite easy to tread on them. That wakes them up with a fright and they give the nearest foot a quick nip. Nurse sharks rarely hurt anyone badly.

A bather's foot dangles dangerously near a nurse shark

THEIR SENSES

Scientists have found that sharks can sense electrical currents. Every living thing gives out an electrical current or pulse. Sharks feel the electrical current through tiny holes, called **pores**, in the skin on their heads. The sharks use the information they receive to find fish to eat. They can even feel the very weak electrical current of a fish or ray buried in sand on the ocean floor.

The pores on the nurse shark's head can be clearly seen

FACT FILE

Common Name: Nurse Shark
Scientific Name: Ginglymostoma cirratum
Color: Yellowish gray
Average Size: Male   – 7 feet, 11 inches
    Female – 8 feet, 1 inch
Where They Live: Seabed, shallow inshore waters
Danger Level: Only attack humans if threatened

WHALE SHARKS

WHALE SHARKS

Whale sharks are the biggest fish in the world. They have often been mistaken for whales because of their enormous size. Whale sharks cruise slowly through the water. They never seem to hurry. Whale sharks have often been seen resting lazily on the surface of the ocean. Today whale sharks are quite rare.

A whale shark swims lazily at the surface

HOW THEY LOOK

Whale sharks have dark green-gray backs with pale yellow spots. Their undersides are white. Whale sharks have broad, flat heads and a very wide mouth. Their huge bodies are rounded, with ridges running from the head to the tail along the back. An average male whale shark is about 27 feet long. The largest whale shark ever known measured over 41 feet long.

Whale sharks have very wide mouths

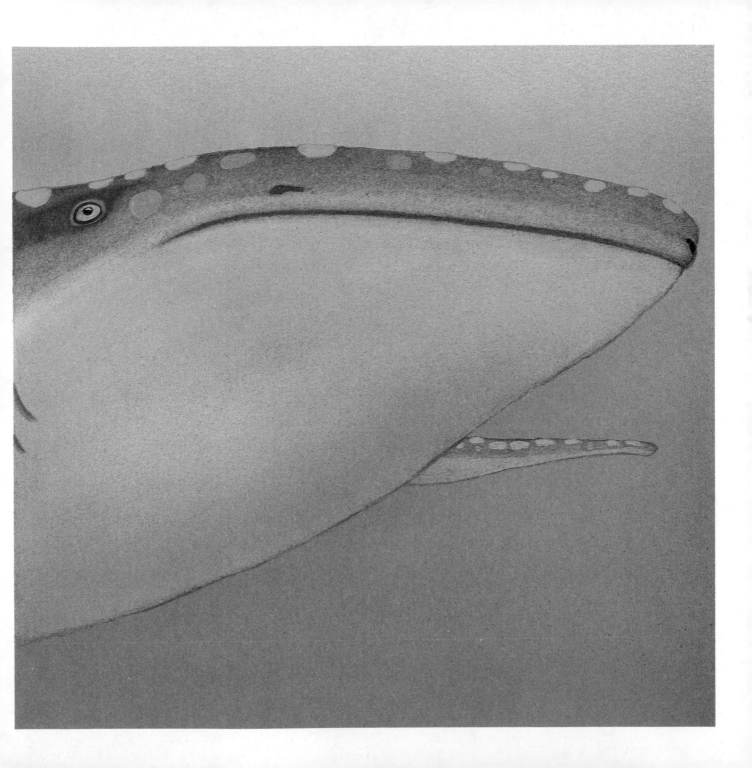

WHERE THEY LIVE

Whale sharks like to live in warm waters. They are found in **tropical oceans**, both far out to sea and near to shore. Whale sharks have been seen along the east coast of the United States and off California. Many whale sharks are found in the Gulf of Mexico at certain times of the year. They are most common in the Indian Ocean.

Whale sharks live in warm waters

WHAT THEY EAT

Whale sharks spend their days feeding on tiny plants called **plankton** and small shrimp-like creatures known as **krill**. They also eat some kinds of fish and squid. The whale sharks open their mouths and swallow whatever goes in. Sometimes they eat garbage by mistake. Buckets, boots, oars, and other such objects have all been found in the stomachs of whale sharks!

Whale sharks eat schools of fish

Whale sharks sometimes eat garbage

Whale sharks are not dangerous

THEIR JAWS AND TEETH

Whale sharks have more than 300 bands of tiny teeth. The teeth are much too small for the sharks to eat very big fish, and the whale sharks' mouths do not open wide enough. The sharks feed on plankton and krill, which they take into their mouths with the sea water. The water is pushed out through the whale sharks' **gill slits**, leaving the food in their mouths to be swallowed.

Whale sharks have many small teeth

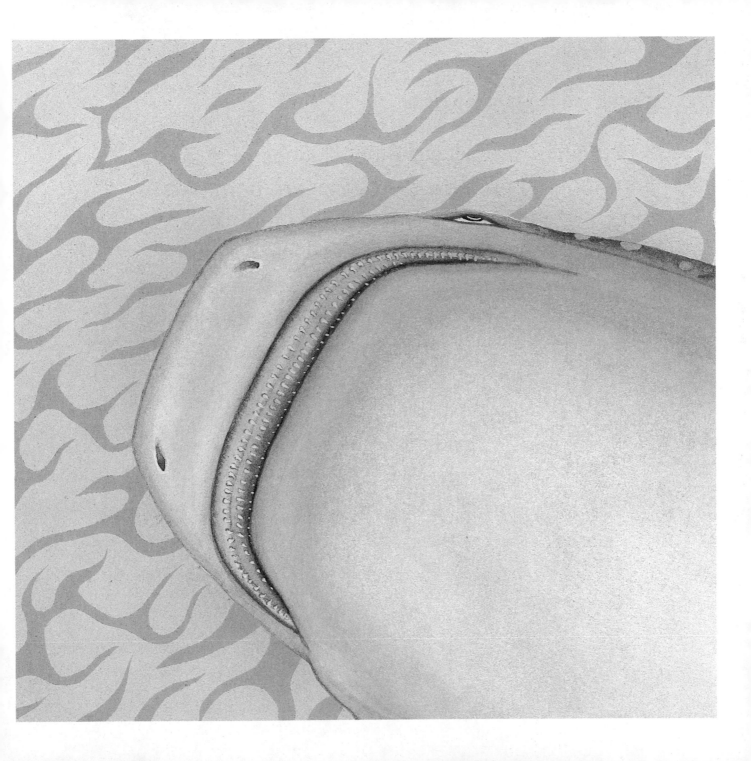

BABY WHALE SHARKS

Scientists are still studying all kinds of sharks to learn more about how the babies are born. We know that the mother whale shark produces oblong-shaped eggs. The baby whale sharks grow inside the eggs. After the eggs are laid, the baby sharks hatch from them. People have found some whale sharks' eggs that were nearly 20 inches long.

Baby whale sharks hatch from eggs

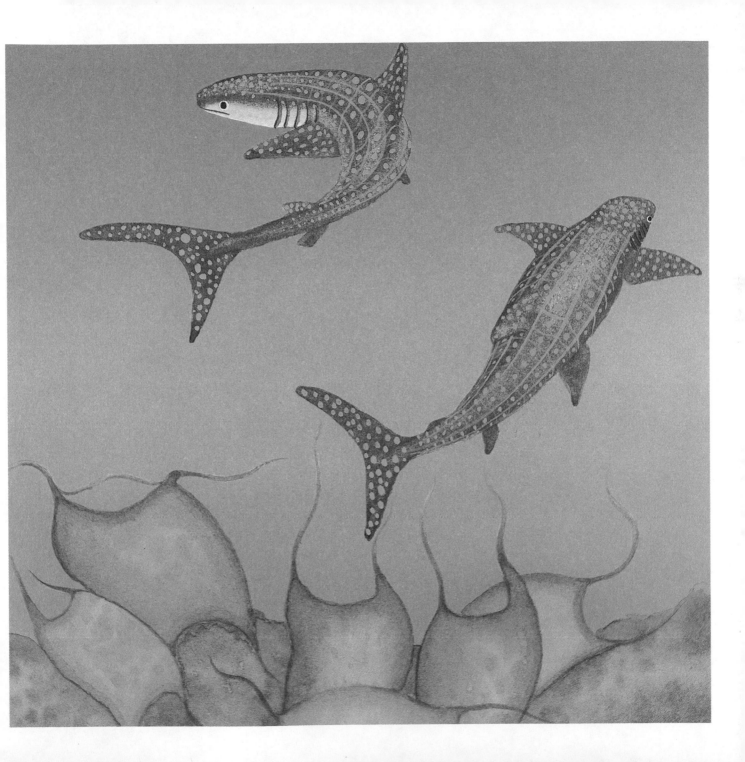

WHALE SHARKS AND MAN

In spite of their size, the huge whale sharks are quite harmless. Their sharp little teeth could hurt you if you were not careful, but whale sharks are not at all **aggressive**. They seem to like people and play happily with them in the water. Whale sharks let divers hold onto their fins and take a ride through the water. They are very gentle when they play.

Whale sharks sometimes give divers rides on their fins

THEIR SKIN

Sharks' skin is covered with scales, which are sometimes called **denticles**. Each kind of shark has differently shaped scales. Scientists can tell what kind of shark they are looking at by the scaly skin. The scales, or denticles, grow backward along the body, much like fur on an animal. If you stroke a shark's body from front to back, it feels smooth. But if you rub it the other way, it is very rough and hurts your hand.

Sharks' skin is made of scales called denticles

FACT FILE

Common Name:	Whale Shark
Scientific Name:	Rhiniodon typus
Color:	Greenish gray with yellow spots
Average Size:	Male – 29 feet, 6 inches
	Female – 26 feet, 3 inches
Where They Live:	Warm waters, inshore and oceans
Danger Level:	No danger

THRESHER SHARKS

THRESHER SHARKS

Thresher sharks take their name from their long tail fins, which lash through the water. The upper part, or **lobe**, of the tail fin is longer than that of any other shark. It sometimes grows to be as long as the body of the shark itself. These tails make thresher sharks some of the easiest sharks to recognize.

Thresher sharks have very long tail fins

HOW THEY LOOK

The largest thresher shark known was over 18 feet long. Its weight was probably about half a ton. An average-sized male thresher is about 11 feet long. The females are slightly larger, usually about 15 feet long. Thresher sharks have stout bodies, which are dark blue-gray on their backs and white underneath. Sometimes their skin is slightly mottled. The most noticeable thing about a thresher shark is its long tail fin.

Male and female thresher sharks

WHERE THEY LIVE

Thresher sharks like to live in warm waters. They are often seen in the oceans off Florida and Southern California. Thresher sharks usually stay in deep water and do not come close to shore. Two smaller **species** of thresher sharks, the Smalltooth Thresher and the Bigeye Thresher, are sometimes found in shallower seas.

Thresher sharks usually live in deep water

WHAT THEY EAT

Thresher sharks live on fish. Their diet includes mackerel, herring, shad, and pilchard—each a different kind of fish. Thresher sharks hunt in groups. They follow schools of fish, herding them together with their long tails. Scientists believe that thresher sharks hit and stun the fish with their tail fins to make them easier to catch. Sometimes by mistake they hit birds that skim the surface of the ocean.

Thresher sharks herd a school of fish with their tails

Thresher sharks like warm waters

*Thresher sharks' tail fins should
be avoided!*

THEIR JAWS AND TEETH

Thresher sharks have small, triangular teeth. They are not very dangerous. All sharks have five or more sets of teeth in their mouth, but only one set that you can see. The rest are folded down inside their mouths. When a shark loses or breaks a tooth, another one grows up to replace it. A shark may go through a hundred sets of teeth in its lifetime.

Thresher sharks have small triangular teeth

BABY THRESHER SHARKS

Female thresher sharks give birth to live young. They swim to a place they know to be safe for the babies while they are small. The water must be warm and have enough food for the young sharks. The mother shark must be careful, because the baby sharks will have to look after themselves from the moment they are born. Each year a female thresher will bear two to four babies. At birth the babies are 4 or 5 feet long.

Baby thresher sharks take care of themselves as soon as they are born

SHARK ATTACK!

Not all sharks are dangerous. Thresher sharks are one of the harmless species of sharks. There are no known cases where threshers have attacked humans. Probably the most dangerous part of a thresher shark is its strong tail fin. If you were hit by that, it would be like being whipped with something very sharp.

Thresher sharks are not dangerous

THEIR SENSES

Most sharks do not have very good hearing. Their ears are more important for balance and finding direction. An extra sense called the **lateralis system** helps sharks find **prey** on which to feed. As well as hearing the movement of fish close by, sharks can feel their **vibrations** through their lateralis systems. This means that they can attack their prey faster.

Thresher sharks use their lateralis system to find food

FACT FILE

Common Name: Thresher Shark
Scientific Name: Aliopas vulpinas
Color: Dark blue-gray
Average Size: Male   – 11 feet, 9 inches
                  Female – 15 feet, 1 inch
Where They Live: Warm waters, offshore
Danger Level: No danger

GLOSSARY

aggressive (ag GRES sive) — likely to attack

carnivorous (car NIV or ous) — flesh-eating

denticles (DEN ti cles) — scales on a shark's back

dorsal fins (DOR sal FINS) — fins on a shark's back

krill (KRILL) — tiny shrimp-like creatures on which sharks feed

lateralis system (lat er AL is SYS tem) — a sense which helps
  sharks find objects by feeling their movements

lobes (LOBES) — the fleshy part of a shark's tail fin

gills (GILLS) — parts of a fish's body that take oxygen from the
  water for it to breathe

nocturnal (noc TUR nal) — active at night

pectoral fins (PEC tor al) — lower fins

plankton (PLANK ton) — tiny plants on which sharks feed

pores (PORES) — tiny openings on the surface of the skin

reefs (REEFS) — chains of rocks or sand close to the surface of the ocean

schools (SCHOOLS) — large groups of sharks, or fish

seabed (SEA bed) — the floor of the ocean

serrated (ser RAT ed) — notched, like the edge of a saw

species (SPE cies) — a scientific term meaning kind or type

to migrate (MI grate) — to move from one place to another, usually at the same time each year

to prey (PREY) — to hunt for food

tropical oceans (TRO pi cal OC eans) — warm seas close to the equator

vibrations (vi BRA tions) — sounds or movements that can be felt

victim (VIC tim) — an injured person